How to Be
TOLERANT

A Question and Answer Book About Tolerance

by Emily James

raintree
a Capstone company — publishers for children

Are all of your friends exactly like you?

Do they have the same hair colour?

Do they have the same types of

families and the same beliefs?

Of course not!

Being tolerant means respecting
the differences between people.

There are many ways
to be tolerant.

Lucy is a new pupil. At the bus stop, Aylah notices she looks lonely.

What should Aylah do to show tolerance?

Aylah invites Lucy to wait with her.

Being kind to someone new shows tolerance.

What can you do to show kindness to a new pupil?

Wyatt and Eli are playing
a word game. Wyatt is slow at first.

What can Eli do
to show tolerance?

Eli is patient.

Understanding that everyone works at a different speed shows tolerance.

How can you be understanding?

Kate's favourite school subject is maths.

Adam is having trouble with his maths homework.

What can Kate do to show tolerance?

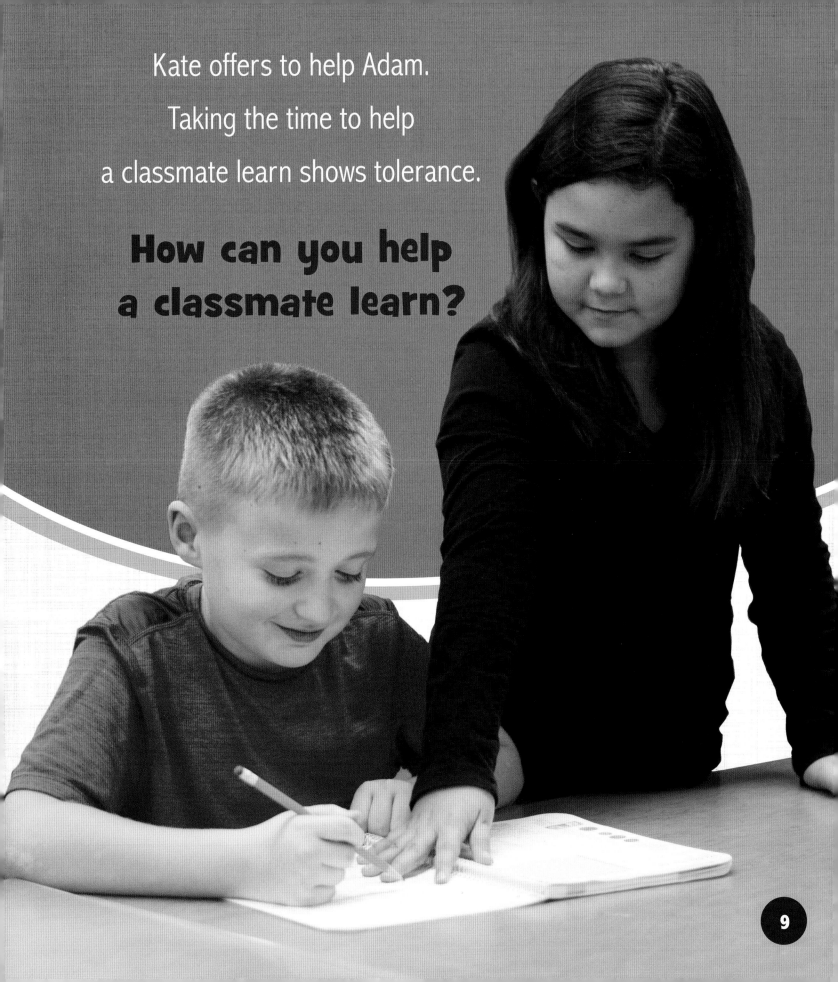

Kate offers to help Adam.
Taking the time to help
a classmate learn shows tolerance.

**How can you help
a classmate learn?**

Ava and Amy start a club for girls only.

Owen asks if he can join their club.

What should Ava and Amy do to show tolerance?

Ava and Amy change the rules
so Owen can join. Including
everyone in a group shows tolerance.

How can you include others?

Dominic lives with his mum and dad.

Charlotte lives with her two mums.

How can the families show tolerance?

The families spend time together.

There are many different types of families.

Accepting other people's differences shows tolerance.

In what ways can you accept other people's differences?

Gavin accidentally breaks Nora's toy.

How can Nora show tolerance?

Nora doesn't get upset. Never treat
someone badly because of a mistake.

How can you show tolerance when someone makes a mistake?

Hannah's family celebrates Christmas.

Evan's family celebrates Hanukkah.

How can the families show tolerance?

They join each other for both of the celebrations.

Sharing other people's traditions shows tolerance.

What other traditions have you celebrated?

Sasha is bringing treats for her friends.

Gunner is the only person in the group who is allergic to dairy.

What can Sasha do to show tolerance?

Sasha makes sure she brings treats that Gunner can eat. Being respectful of someone's differences shows tolerance.

What can you do to be respectful of someone's differences?

19

Marco is excited to run around at the park.

Kya trips over her untied shoelace.

How can Marco show tolerance?

Marco helps Kya tie her shoelace.

Being patient is part of being tolerant.

Can you think
of a time when
you had to
be patient?

Anna and Sasha are friends.

Anna loves cheering for her favourite sports team.

Sasha is a fan of another team.

How can the girls show tolerance?

They listen to each other's views.

Respecting other people's

opinions shows tolerance.

How can you respect people's views?

Levi's classmates are playing catch.

Levi is in a wheelchair.

How can his classmates show tolerance?

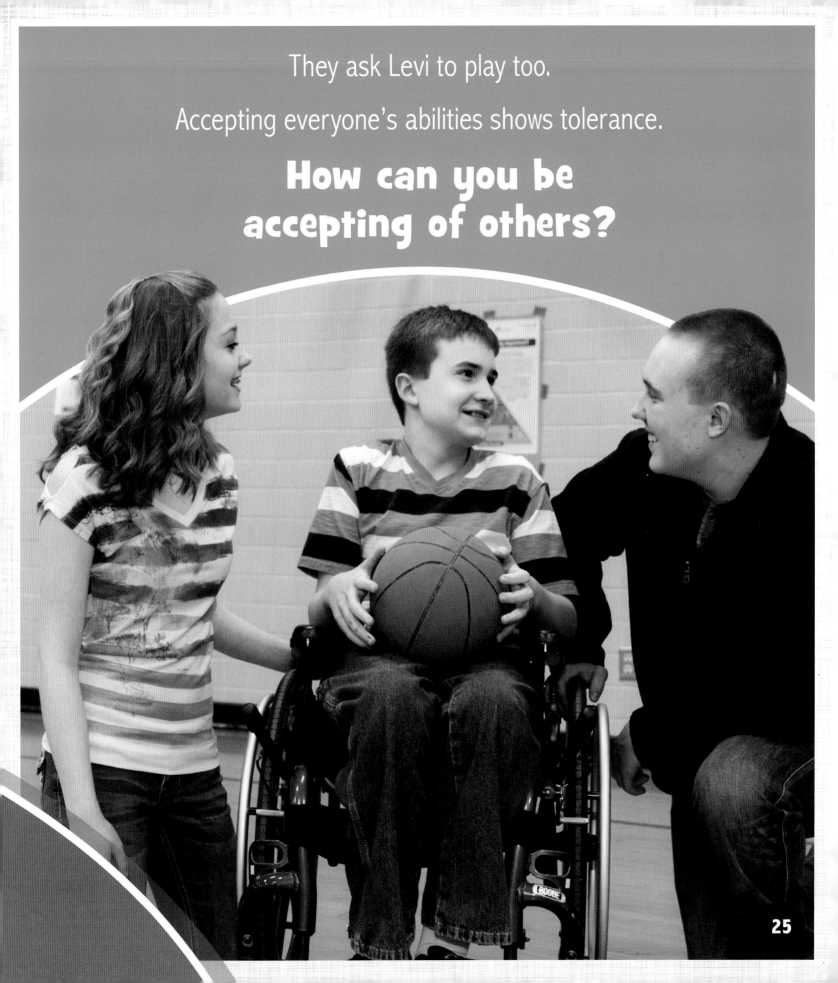

They ask Levi to play too.

Accepting everyone's abilities shows tolerance.

How can you be accepting of others?

Maria is new to the country. She dresses differently from some of the other children.

What could other children do to show tolerance?

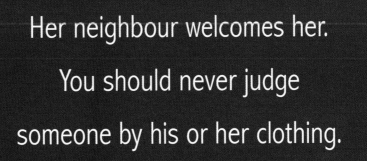

Her neighbour welcomes her.
You should never judge
someone by his or her clothing.

**How could you welcome
a new friend?**

Olivia has to get glasses.

She is worried her friends will make fun of her.

What should her friends do to show tolerance?

Olivia's friends tell her the glasses look great!
Treating others the way you would
want to be treated shows tolerance.

How do you treat others?

Glossary

ability skill

accidentally without meaning to

allergic when something makes someone feel ill after eating, touching or breathing it

celebrate to do something fun on a special day

opinion a person's ideas and beliefs about something

patient staying calm during frustrating times

tolerance understanding that your way isn't the only way

tradition a custom, idea or belief passed down through time

Comprehension questions

1. Owen wants to join Ava and Amy's club. What do Ava and Amy do?

2. Can you think of a time when you showed tolerance? What did you do?

3. Marco and Eli both showed tolerance by being patient. What does it mean to be patient? Hint: Use your glossary!

Find out more

Books

How Should I Behave?, Mick Manning and Brita Granstrom (Franklin Watts, 2017)

I Am Kind (My Behaviour), Liz Lennon (Franklin Watts, 2015)

What Does it Mean to be British?, Nick Hunter (Raintree, 2017)

Websites

bbc.co.uk/education/topics/zw339j6/resources/1
Find lots of videos showing how you can be a good citizen in many different ways.

bbc.co.uk/education/topics/z&rrd2p/resources/1
Watch videos about accepting people's differences.

Index

Raintree is an imprint of Capstone Global Library Limited, a company incorporated in England and Wales having its registered office at 264 Banbury Road, Oxford, OX2 7DY – Registered company number: 6695582

www.raintree.co.uk
myorders@raintree.co.uk

Text © Capstone Global Library Limited 2018
The moral rights of the proprietor have been asserted.

ISBN 978 1 4747 4388 4
21 20 19 18 17
10 9 8 7 6 5 4 3 2 1

British Library Cataloguing in Publication Data
A full catalogue record for this book is available from the British Library.

Acknowledgements
All photographs by Capstone Studio/Karon Dubke, except:
Shutterstock: RoyStudioEU throughout, (background texture)

Editorial Credits
Jaclyn Jaycox, editor; Heidi Thompson, designer; Jo Miller, media researcher; Laura Manthe, production specialist; Marcy Morin, scheduler